The
Long-Nosed
Rooter

ISBN 978-1-68570-976-1 (paperback)
ISBN 978-1-68570-977-8 (digital)

Christian Faith Publishing
832 Park Avenue
Meadville, PA 16335
www.christianfaithpublishing.com

Printed in the United States of America

The Long-Nosed Rooter

Anna Pendergrass

My family has been telling the story about the Long-Nosed Rooter for a very long time. My dad told me, his parents told him, and all their parents told them. You get the idea. It's an old story, and everybody tells it a little differently. Everyone adds their own opinions and spins. But make no mistake; it's about the same beady-eyed, Long-Nosed Rooter! No one is sure exactly how everything happened; maybe Mr. Samuels was having a nightmare. He had bad dreams every time he ate potted meat and sauerkraut out of a can. He knew he had eaten a lot of that these days. The story was about some kind of animal, I guess.

The story began with a guy named Tom Samuels. He had a wife and two children, two boys. Every day they prayed for the Lord's protection, a way to support the family, and to have a place to live of their own. Their needs were simple.

Mr. Samuels had an old rusty 1948 Chevrolet. It sputtered and missed, but so far, it had gotten him headed for an old home place way out in the countryside in Pikeville, Tennessee. Mr. Samuels is what you'd call homeless. Today his family is staying with his mother in a community there called Beaver Hill.

Mr. Samuels had a hopeful look on his face as he spread dust from behind on that old, narrow, winding, dusty road. It was washboardy and full of potholes. But at the end of the road stood an old house no one had lived in for years. Mr. Samuels was told that anyone who could spend the night there could have the old home place for their own. Mr. Samuels was assured by a reliable source—the owner, Jack Wilson—that the farm was for the taking to the brave person who could make it through the night at the old homeplace. Mr. Samuels wondered why someone had not already snatched it up.

"That person must stay without running away till the sun comes up the next day," the contract read. Old Man Wilson, having no family around, held up a yellowed and dog-eared contract that had been notarized for proof of his intentions to give away the property. Briars and vines had grown up around the old house, but Mr. Samuels thought the place had potential to be a nice little produce farm. Mr. Samuels could see in his head beautiful red and yellow apples and rosy-orange peaches growing on trees. He could imagine row after row of vegetables growing on the land. It had a few acres of woods and fields around it. There was even a small pond in one of the fields.

The wind had started to whistle, and it had started to snow. My goodness! It was sure getting cold just as it was getting dark and just when he finally arrived at the old house on the hill.

The old house was fairly large but run down. It had no power or furniture, and some of the old caulked windows had cracks and holes in them. There was an old potbellied stove near an old stone chimney. He was glad to see a large stack of wood that had not been used. He soon had a fire going. He gathered up some leaves that had blown through the windows over time and fashioned them into a makeshift mattress. He had brought a few old patchwork quilts his family had been using in the car. He suddenly realized he was getting kind of sleepy. It had been a long day finding this place.

10

He poked the fire up, yawned loudly, and scratched his back as he usually did each night, readying for bed. He would sleep in his clothes to stay warmer. He lay down and soon was asleep. A little while later, he woke up, feeling as though he was freezing! He was lying at the bottom of the porch steps, in the yard out in the snow! He thought wildly, *What just happened?* He ran up the steps and opened the squeaking door… *Eeerk! eekk!* He closed it back as soon as he could. He poked up the fire, put another log in the stove, warmed his backside, warmed his front side, then scratched his back like he does each night before he goes to bed yawning. He again fell asleep soundly.

Once again, he woke up lying in the snow, freezing! Again, he thought, *What has happened? How did I get here again? This time I'm going to find out!* So he ran back up the steps, sprinted back through the squeaky door, and slammed it closed. He poked up the fire, put on another log, and warmed himself all over, turning around like a chicken on a rotisserie. He thought, *This time, old Samuels has a plan!* After scratching his back like he did each night, he covered himself back up in his makeshift bed. He started to go back to sleep.

But this time was different. Mr. Samuels decided he would just pretend to be asleep. He squinted his eyes almost shut and waited to see what would happen. After a while, he heard the squeaky door. *Eeark!* He thought he heard light footsteps getting closer. Soon he saw a wooly, long-nosed creature peeking down at him with its beady red eyes! It was the Long-Nosed Rooter! The old critter was breathing down on Mr. Samuels. It bowed its long gnarly head, tucking its tushes under Mr. Samuels. It would quickly scamper around to look Samuels straight in the

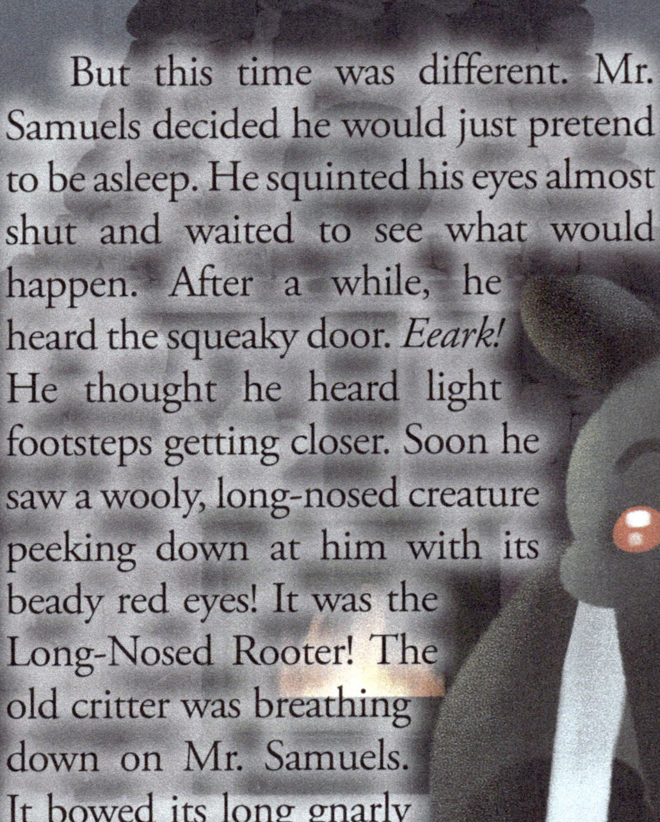

eyes to see if Mr. Samuels was still asleep. Then he would roll Samuels further toward the door with his big, long tushes. Closer, closer to the door he rolled Mr. Samuels. He checked a last time as he rolled Mr. Samuels out the front door to the porch. The snow was getting deep now, the Long-Nosed Rooter pitched Samuels over the edge of the porch into a big snowdrift with its long tushes!

This time Mr. Samuels saw it happening, jumped up screaming at the surprised Long-Nosed Rooter! The Long Nosed Rooter tried to slide under a loose board on the porch but was blocked by a long limb that had fallen from a tree. Mr. Samuels was using it for a tool to capture the critter. The critter's eyes grew big and alarmed-looking as Mr. Samuels chased it around and around and around the old house! The Long-Nosed Rooter, whatever it was, made a break for the woods.

Mr. Samuels dusted off his hands and sighed with relief. He ran back up the squeaky steps, closed the squeaky door, poked up the fire, and put another log on the fire. He scratched his back and crawled back in his leaf-filled makeshift mattress with the patchwork quilts, and soon fell back to sleep again. When he woke back up the next morning, his eyes widened with excitement. He made it through the night! Samuels scratched his head and wondered if he had been dreaming. Regardless, he knew the old house and property was his! The Long-Nosed Rooter never came to the old house again.

Mr. Samuels and his family fixed up the old place and had a nice place to live out in the country. He got a job at a local sawmill. He and his wife, Ruth, made a garden. Their boys, John and George, fished from the pond and hunted in the woods. On the side, Mr. Samuels took a job running critters out of people's houses. For some reason, he was good at that. Mrs. Samuels was able to stay home with the boys, attend their social functions, work her garden, and can or freeze her produce grown in her garden. This was something she had always dreamed of doing. Mr. and Mrs. Samuels enjoyed John's football and baseball games. They enjoyed attending George's golf and cross-country competitions. They found a good church about a mile down the road. They frequently had outings on the farm with neighbors and friends. They were all very thankful each day they had been blessed with answered prayers. Home sweet home!

THE END

What Bible Lesson was This?

Therefore take no thought, say, What shall we eat? Or, What shall we drink? Or, Wherewithal shall we be clothed?

—Matthew 6:31

The Lord knows we need all these basic things.

But seek ye first the kingdom of God, and his righteousness; and all these things shall be added unto you.

—Matthew 6:33

It may not be exactly what we want, but our needs SHALL be provided. The Bible tells us.

Ask, and it shall be given you; seek, and ye shall find; knock, and it shall be opened unto you.

—Matthew 7:7

For everyone that asketh receiveth; and he that seeketh findeth; and to him that knocketh it shall be opened.

—Matthew 7:8 (KJV Bible verses)

We need to be so thankful for all the things the Lord allows us to have. If we learn about him and put our full trust in him, he will do even greater things for us. He will save us and give us eternal life!

will be dedicating this book to my husband, Eugene Pendergrass, now deceased, who was always encouraging me to submit my work for publication.

About the Author

Anna Pendergrass is a retired teacher, having worked with grades K–12. She has been a Sunday school teacher for over forty years, working with youth from their toddler ages through high school ages. She has taught in public schools and in correctional settings.

Anna has earned degrees in education and in special education from Tennessee Tech University. She has also received highly qualified status in social studies.

She loves the Lord Jesus Christ and enjoys going to church, being with family, gardening, and writing and singing congregational music, stories, and poetry. She loves her pets and all animals in God's creation. She comes from a large family in a small town where everybody knows everybody and has kinship with most of them in some way. The rest of Bledsoe County and surrounding counties are beloved neighbors and friends (or will be as soon as she meets them) because she loves everyone.